Air, Sun, and Water

How Weather Works

DEVELOPED IN COOPERATION
WITH
THE FRANKLIN INSTITUTE
PHILADELPHIA, PENNSYLVANIA

Copyright © 1993 by Scholastic Inc.   All rights reserved. Published by Scholastic Inc.   Printed in the U.S.A.
ISBN 0-590-26135-5
1 2 3 4 5 6 7 8 9 10   09   99 98 97 96 95 94 93 92

THE EARTH, WITHIN THE UNIVERSE, IS CONSTANTLY CHANGING.

Air, Sun, and Water

The sun, air, and water make weather,
which can be observed and measured.

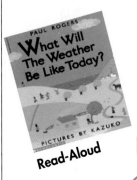

PAUL ROGERS
What Will The Weather Be Like Today?
PICTURES BY KAZUKO

Read-Aloud

VIDEO

Air, Sun, and Water

Weather is the condition of the surrounding air.

What Is the Weather Like? **4**

How Do You Know Air Is There? **6**

Does Air Take Up Space? **8**

The sun heats the air, which moves, changes direction, and moves other things.

What Makes Air Feel Hot or Cold? **10**

What Makes Air Move? **12**

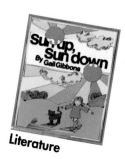

Literature

How Hard Can the Wind Blow?......................**14**

Which Way Does the Wind Blow?...................**16**

The sun heats water and makes it move through the water cycle.

What Else Is Part of Weather? **18**

Does Water Move? **20**

Literature

What Does the Sun Do to Water? **22**

What Happens to Water in the Air? **24**

What Makes Rain Fall? **26**

What Are Snow and Frost? **28**

What Did We Learn?

What Is the Weather Like
Where You Live?..............................**30**

Glossary **32**

What Is the Weather Like?

How can you find out?

Be a weather scientist.

You need:
Markers or
crayons

❶ Go outside.

❷ What weather clues do you see?
What weather clues do you hear?
What weather clues do you feel?
Draw or write about them.

What difference does weather make?
Can people go swimming here?

How will the weather affect this game?

THINK!
How does knowing about the weather help you?

How will the weather affect these oranges?

5

How Do You Know Air Is There?

Weather is made up of air and sun and water.
What weather clues did you find?

You can see sun and water, but where is air?
How do you know it's there?

Look at the pictures. Look around you.
Where is air?

Prove air is there.

You need:
Plastic bag
Twist tie

1 Catch some air in a bag.

2 Tie the bag closed.

3 Squeeze it! Blow it! Press it! Toss it! What happens?

4 Open the bag. Now squeeze it. What happens to the air?

THINK!
Is there air inside you? Where?

Does Air Take Up Space?

Air is all around. You caught some in your bag. You can't see air, but you can find out more about it.

Experiment with air.

You need:
Plastic bag
Plastic bottle
Tape

❶ Tape the bags to the bottle.

❷ What do you think will happen if you push down on one bag?

What happens? What does this tell you about air?

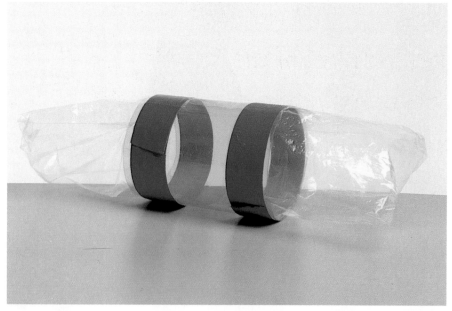

The earth has a blanket of air all around. You breathe the air that's all around.

Weather happens in the air all around.

THINK!
What can you do to make something different happen with the bottle?

What Makes Air Feel Hot or Cold?

You know that air is part of weather. What makes air get hotter or colder? How can you find out?

You need:
Thermometers
Masking tape
String

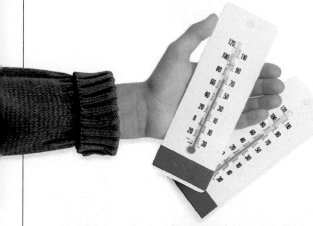

Use a thermometer.

1 What do the red lines tell you? Mark them with tape.

2 Hang one thermometer in the sun. Hang one in the shade. Wait.

3 What happened to the red lines? Mark them with tape. Where is the air warmer? Why?

When the sun warms the earth, the air around the earth gets warm, too. Look at these pictures. Do you think the air is hot or cold?

THINK!
What happens to the air at night?

What Makes Air Move?

Can you observe moving air?

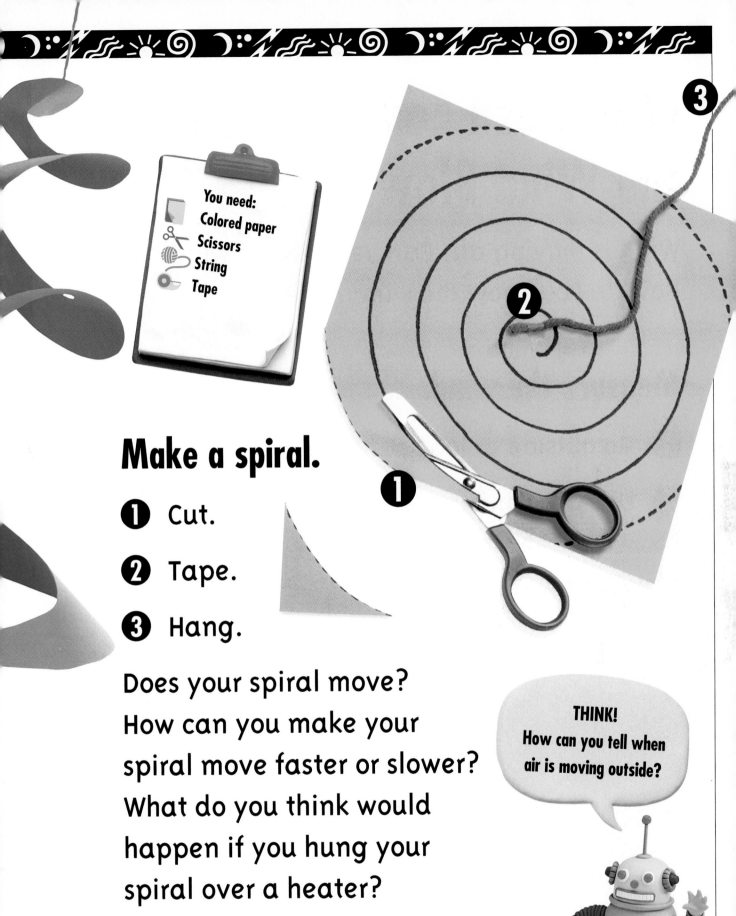

You need:
Colored paper
Scissors
String
Tape

Make a spiral.

1 Cut.

2 Tape.

3 Hang.

Does your spiral move?
How can you make your
spiral move faster or slower?
What do you think would
happen if you hung your
spiral over a heater?

The sun's heat makes air move.
What do you call moving air?

THINK!
How can you tell when
air is moving outside?

How Hard Can the Wind Blow?

Wind is moving air. Can you see the wind? How do you know the wind is there?

Measure the wind.

1 Go outside or look out the window.

2 Use this wind scale to measure the wind. How hard is the wind blowing now?

Wind Scale

0. Calm — Smoke goes up
1. Light air — Smoke drifts
2. Light breeze — Leaves rustle
3. Gentle breeze — Flags flap
4. Moderate breeze — Paper flies
5. Fresh breeze — Lakes get choppy
6. Strong breeze — Large branches move

Wind is a part of weather. The wind can move clouds across the sky or blow very hard during a storm.

THINK!
How do people use wind?

What Else Is Part of Weather?

Air and sun help make weather.
Find out what else is in weather.

Make a weather cup.

You need:
Plastic cups
Soil
Seeds
Water
Tape
Pencil

❶ Put soil in one cup.
Make a hole in the soil
with your pencil.

❷ Put the seeds in the
hole and cover them.
Water the seeds.

How is this weather like the weather inside your cup?

THINK!
What will happen if you leave your weather cup uncovered?

3 Put the other cup on top. Tape them together. Set the weather cup in the sun.

Does Water Move?

Water is part of weather. Tell about the weather where you live. Where is water in your weather? How does water get into the weather?

You need:
Water
Colored paper

Make a water painting.

1 Dip your finger in the water.

2 Draw with your finger on the paper.

What do you think will happen to the water on your water painting?

What happened in this picture? How will the ground get dry?

What Does the Sun Do to Water?

Water can evaporate, or move into the air. The water from the paintings evaporated into the air. What makes water evaporate faster?

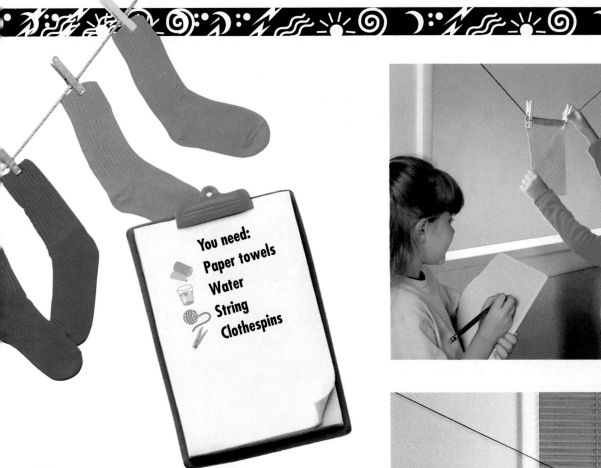

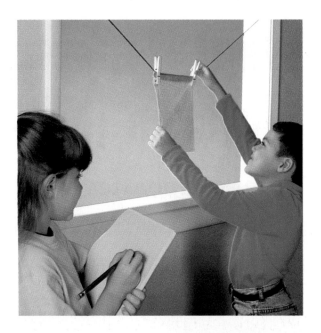

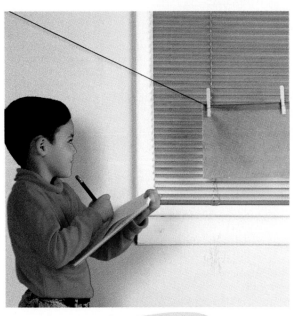

You need:
Paper towels
Water
String
Clothespins

Test evaporation.

❶ Wet two paper towels.

❷ Hang one towel in the warm sun. Hang one in the cooler shade.

❸ What do you predict will happen? Check the towels every ten minutes.

Is there a difference between the towels? What do you think happened?

THINK!
Does the sun change water temperature? How can you test it?

What Happens to Water in the Air?

Water evaporates into the air. The water in the air is water vapor. There is always water vapor in the air, but you can't see it.

Sometimes warm air with lots of water vapor rises. As it meets colder air, tiny water drops can form. Then you can see the water in the air. Clouds are water drops in the air.

You need:
Two cans
Ice
Warm water
Masking tape
Marker

Make a cloud.

❶ Fill one can with warm water and one with ice. Label the cans.

❷ Hold the can with ice above the can with warm water.

❸ Write what happens. What do you think made it happen? ✏️

Ice

Water

THINK!
What happens when you breathe out warm air on a cold day?

What Makes Rain Fall?

You saw clouds form from water vapor.
How do clouds turn into rain?

High above the earth the air is cold.
Warm moist air rises from the earth.

As warm moist air meets cold air, clouds can form.
Clouds are made up of tiny water drops.
More and more water drops form and join together.

Rain falls when water drops get bigger and heavier.

What Are Snow and Frost?

Sometimes a cloud is so cold that water vapor changes into snowflakes instead of into raindrops. Then snow falls.

Frost is like snow, but it forms near the ground instead of in clouds.

You need:
Metal can
Ice
Salt

Make some frost in a can.

❶ Wipe the can dry and put ice in it.

❷ Pour salt over the ice. Wait ten minutes.

❸ Look again in a little while. What do you see now?

THINK!
How do farmers protect their crops from frost?

What Is the Weather Like Where You Live?

Weather is a system made up of air and sun and water. What is your weather like? Is it the same every day? Is it the same all year? Think about winter.

In Seattle winter is rainy.

In St. Paul winter is snowy.

In Los Angeles winter is warm and sunny.

In Miami winter i hot and damp.

You need:
Construction
paper
Markers or
crayons
Tape or glue
Scissors
Paper fastener

In Boston
winter is
icy cold.

Make a weather wheel to
tell about your weather.
What is the air like?
What is the sun like?
Where is the water?

What do you like best about
the weather where you live?

Clouds: Clouds are made up of water droplets or ice crystals. Clouds can form when warm air with lots of water vapor meets cold air.

Evaporate: When water evaporates, it changes to gas and moves into the air. The sun makes water evaporate faster.

Frost: Frost forms when water vapor changes to tiny ice crystals. Frost is like snow, but it forms near the ground.

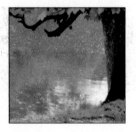

Rain: Rain forms when water vapor in clouds changes to water droplets. Rain falls when the water droplets join together.

Snow: Snow is frozen water vapor. When the air around a cloud is very cold, water vapor changes to snowflakes.

Temperature: Temperature is how hot or cold something is. Air temperature changes during the day.